Chakras

A Comprehensive Manual On Utilizing Mantras And Frequencies To Achieve Chakra Healing Through The Practice Of Sound Healing And Chakra Balancing

(A Comprehensive Manual For The Restoration Of Your Chakras And Harmonization Of Your Energy By Means Of Heightened Consciousness)

Sebastian Mullen

TABLE OF CONTENT

Introduction 1

Sacral Chakra: Basis And Healing 15

Mistakes To Avoid When Attempting To Heal The Sacral Chakra 27

Methods For Chakra Healing And Balancing 40

Throat Chakra Healing 60

Chakra Sacral 74

Crown Chakra Healing And Balancing Techniques: 81

The Throat Chakra Is Known As Vishuddhi. 115

Yoga Poses For Heart Chakra Balance 149

Ego Destroyer 157

Introduction

Welcome to a Transformative, Powerful Encounter

You are about to start on a tremendous new healing adventure. One that will have an impact on all aspects of your life. You may not know the energy centers within, around, and above you. Still, they exist and impact your physical, mental, emotional, and spiritual well-being. The best location to start any new spiritual journey is within yourself. Learning about your chakras is a spiritual journey. It delves far beyond the physical element of your existence and into the very depths of your existence—your soul, purpose, and capacity to live a genuinely amazing life.

Within your grasp is a vast, powerful, energy-linked vortex linked to the entire cosmos. It is linked to your energetic system, comprised of chakras. It may be beyond your current ability to fully comprehend your powerful connection to the entire Universe (especially if this is a new concept to you). Still, it is present within your body's energy centers. When you connect to these energy vortexes and learn how to keep them flowing, you will have greater personal empowerment and deeper connectivity.

Healing and understanding how to use your chakra system's strength can also connect you to your higher self, sometimes known as your "soul self." True empowerment is found in our authenticity, which depends on how open your energy system is to receiving sustenance from the subtle energy of your soul. Everything you need to continue in your spiritual and emotional journey is your ability to mend the energy flow within your physical existence. The goal of this book is to assist you in accomplishing just that. Understanding your full chakra system and how to connect to it will provide you with the tools you need to live a more fulfilling spiritual life.

Cleaning and mending your chakra system daily or monthly will provide you with a life of greater attentiveness and many spiritual awakenings. It will also assist you in reaching your full potential and experiencing genuine happiness. We live in a time when information overload can make it difficult to understand what success and happiness should look like in our lives. Spirituality frequently takes a back place in an age of commercialization and materialism. This is unfortunate since this is not the way to find enduring happiness. Many people lose themselves daily because they are separated from their souls.

If you don't make a concerted effort to live a cleaner, more holistic lifestyle that includes regular chakra healing, the distance will get wider, which is bad for your health. Clearing blocked energy from your chakras reduces stress, sharpens your intuition, and increases your immune system and your power. This is why I've decided to join the world's rising healing movement to make a significant spiritual difference. Healing Your Chakras can bring you closer to experiencing genuine success, happiness, and more delightful moments. On a spiritual level, you will truly discover who you are; this is where your authentic power rests!

How will we BE when we genuinely understand that we are all one?

However, the worst thing we can do for the world is not truly love or blame ourselves because our lack of love spreads like a tsunami through our encounters with others.

Tantra teaches us that we are perfectly capable of accepting ourselves. This is both the first and last step on the Awakening route. That is why forgiveness rituals such as Ho'oponopono always begin with forgiving ourselves for anything that is out of balance inside us.

When we get to the section discussing the spiral model of meditation, the Snail's Shell, I'll go over this point further.

When you truly understand what it means, if the ancient tantric declared that everything is connected to everything, the ability to forgive (self-) becomes extremely vital.

All of us are murderers.

One Kashmiri tantra instructor began a seminar in Zurich many years ago with the bold words "We are all murderers here," which I attended at the time.

They did not mean that we had all physically killed someone or committed a crime in our lives. But, simply by being present and a member of our society, we are indirectly complicit in the suffering of people, animals, and the environment. Furthermore, many of us may have had violent desires toward someone with whom we disagreed at some point in our lives, even if we did not act on them (hopefully).

For example, I recall having violent fantasies in my adolescence, such as when a car narrowly missed running me over in a crosswalk, and I wished the driver, if not death, then at least a good smash-up.

Everything is interconnected.

Even if a person has had a deep dedication to nonviolence since childhood, he or she is likely to have watched a movie or television series depicting violence and so been a participant, at least mentally, in the events depicted.

Our taxes in many nations subsidize the development of weapons of war that cause agony somewhere in the world. Except for pure vegans, almost all of us benefit in some way from the fact that so-called animals have long been viewed and handled as products rather than as independent living creatures.

Numerous other examples exist of how we are interwoven with everything our society does. I believe you understand what I mean.

We can draw two key conclusions from this.

First and foremost, let us refrain from passing judgment on others.

Second, let us not condemn ourselves because we have little influence over anything, even our acts. The only thing we can train ourselves to have a lot of influence over is our own experience, the way we perceive things.

Is this difficult to accept? Don't worry; it will all become evident once we begin the workouts.

Let me elaborate on the second remark, which may not be clear initially. Close observation of our subconscious patterns and shadows takes most meditation practitioners to at least a partial realization that we have very limited control over our actions.

This is because they are heavily influenced by the same subconscious conditionings, habits, and imprints often formed during early childhood. In my book, The Power of Sankalpa, I go into much greater depth on how this works.

Just the following: Our free will is only (relatively) free when we can be truly present and so become sensitive to impulses for action that do not stem from habit but from our higher self—also known as our inspiration.

And, as you might expect, meditation comes in handy again in this search.

However, the objective is not that we are doing something "wrong" and must now meditate to break free of our conditioning and act more freely and generously. In most situations, this is a genuine and pleasant side effect of the practice. However, as long as we are in this body on Earth, it is unlikely that we will be able to entirely free ourselves from our conditioned acts.

No, we can teach ourselves to have more control over the quality of our experiences and how we see and judge things. To become increasingly visible.To be more spontaneous and direct, and to accept oneself completely.

Let us delve a little deeper into how we work as human beings. The American psychologist Marshall B. Rosenberg invented Nonviolent Communication ("NVC"), providing a useful notion for better understanding our decision-making mechanisms. During the racial turmoil in Detroit, Mr. Rosenberg explored the function of communication in conflict.

If you're wondering what communication has to do with meditation and tantra, consider the following ideas, which offer one possible perspective on meditation and immersion:

Meditation is identical to the practice of living in the present moment.

Being alive entails engaging and relating (both to the outside world and oneself).

Communication is the manifestation of our relationship to something outside of ourselves.

So, life is a form of communication.

Sacral Chakra: Basis And Healing

Lower abdomen, just below the navel

The pelvic cavity, reproductive organs, kidneys, and bladder are all body correspondences. However, blood, lymph, digestive secretions, and sperm are also present.

Corresponding Glands: The sexual organs, including the ovaries and prostate, are the glands for the Sacral Chakra. These organs are in charge of developing male and female sexual traits and regulating the female menstrual cycle.

Taste is a sensory function.

A lotus with six petals is the symbol.

Water is an element.

Vam Mantra

The moon is a planet.

After laying a solid foundation with the root chakra, we move on to the emotional realm with the sacral chakra, also known as Svadhisthana. A balanced sacral chakra helps us feel completely and experience life, whereas the root chakra provides a firm feeling of being. This indicates that after our survival needs are addressed, it is time to pursue delightful hobbies and happiness. We may be ashamed of our feelings, have creative blockages, and struggle to accept our sexuality. So, let us look at how the sacral chakra empowers us in these areas and discover strategies to balance it so we can enjoy life in all itssplendor.

Sacral Chakra – The Most Important Factors

As previously said, the sacral chakra influences crucial parts of our lives, allowing us to feel joy and fulfillment. After all, without the ability to enjoy ourselves, life becomes a tedious routine and an unending list of tasks!

For example, pleasure can lead to fulfillment and happiness. It allows us to feel delight and pursue activities that provide much-needed relief from the stresses of daily life. And the sacral chakra helps this experience by attracting possibilities that boost happy feelings.

And the height of pleasure can be found in sexuality. This is why a healthy sacral chakra is necessary for a fulfilling and safe sexual life. A blocked chakra can cause a lack of sexual desire, whereas an overactive chakra can lead to dangerous or unhealthy sexual activities.

Simultaneously, persons with blocked sacral chakras frequently fail to discover a sense of longing, making it difficult to generate favorable outcomes. An unblocked sacral chakra allows us to access and express our inner aspirations in the physical world.

Humans have a natural impulse to create as well. We all engage in acts of creation at some point, whether in artistic expression or constructing our careers.

On the other hand, the sacral chakra serves as a reservoir of creative energy, allowing us to express ourselves in unique ways. A blocked chakra, on the other hand, can cause stiff and inflexible thinking, making it difficult to express creativity and find satisfaction in the current.

In brief, while other chakras can influence emotions, the sacral chakra is the major center for experiencing and managing our emotional environment and enjoying happy emotions.

Sacral Chakra Blockages: Common Causes

Because the sacral chakra is so directly linked to our emotions, it can get blocked due to various situations and experiences. Here are some of the most popular reasons:

Emotional events such as sorrow, divorce, or family problems can cause an imbalance of emotions and energy blockages. Repressed sentiments or heightened emotional reactivity can result from ineffective coping techniques.

Emotions Denial: Some people assume repressing their emotions will make them disappear. However, suppressing emotions can cause physical and emotional pain because the energy must be released in some way. Recognizing and accepting emotions is essential for a healthy sacral chakra.

Pleasure Denial: Individuals may unknowingly deny themselves pleasure and creativity due to cultural indoctrination or stressful work conditions. Prioritizing work over pleasure can lead to sacral chakra blockage, hindering a balanced and meaningful existence.

Sexual Shame: Feelings of shame over sex can arise from feelings of unworthiness for love or intimacy, which might be influenced by society or family beliefs on the subject. Unhealthy sexual ideas might make it difficult to have satisfying sexual experiences.

Boundaries and safety affect numerous chakras and cause dread of or unfavorable attitudes about sex. Healing from sexual abuse frequently necessitates professional assistance in addition to other healing options.

Please keep in mind that, given the seriousness of some of these situations, particularly sexual abuse, it is strongly advised to get professional help and engage with a mental health expert.

Symptoms of Sacral Chakra Dysfunction

Imbalanced Sacral Chakra: Sacral chakra imbalances are common during puberty when the onset of sexual urges can cause uneasiness. Handling these energies becomes difficult due to a lack of suitable parental supervision and/or parental education. Early childhood experiences of lack of sensitivity and physical connection also contribute to sexual denial and rejection. As a result, these energies' creative potential is lost, and they may be expressed inappropriately, such as through suppressed desires or sexual fantasies. Some people may even turn to sexuality as a form of escape. These imbalances lead to uneasiness, conflicts in romantic relationships, and a tendency to prioritize one's sexual demands. Often, there is a constant desire for a satisfying sexual relationship without realizing that the secret to fulfillment is within oneself.

Sacral Chakra Blockage:

The sacral chakra is commonly blocked as a result of childhood events. You may have missed sensory stimulation, contact, caresses, and tenderness if your parents suppressed their sensuality and sexuality. As a result, you withdrew from this sphere of experience, effectively blocking the rising sexual energy during adolescence. This successful repression results in a loss of self-esteem, confidence, emotional numbness, and a reduced capacity for sexual feelings. In some instances, life may appear dull and uninteresting.

Watch out for these warning signs:

Denial of pleasure and enjoyment.

Disconnection from one's feelings or difficulties expressing and connecting with one's emotions.

Even in the presence of others, I feel a profound sense of isolation and loneliness.

Feeling uninspired, unmotivated, and removed from life's pleasures.

Difficulty developing and sustaining healthy ties and relationships.

Having intense emotional highs and lows, frequently without a clear cause or trigger.

A lack of enthusiasm or zest for life.

Aversion to sex or a poor libido.

Resistance to or fear of change can stifle personal growth and development.

Using drugs or participating in addictive behaviors to alleviate emotional pain or numbness.

Physical Symptoms to Watch For:

Having issues or challenges with sexual functioning or fulfillment.

Lower back pain that is persistent or reoccurring.

Hip pain, stiffness, or discomfort.

Disruptions in renal function.

Premenstrual dysphoria (PMDD) or painful premenstrual symptoms.

Anemia.

Cysts in the ovaries.

You may restore harmony and vigor in these areas by treating and balancing the sacral chakra. However, remember that the above symptoms might vary in severity and can be impacted by personal circumstances. If you have many physical symptoms or recurring issues, don't hesitate to contact your doctor or a mental health expert.

Mistakes To Avoid When Attempting To Heal The Sacral Chakra

And now, here are some frequent sacral chakra healing mistakes to avoid:

Emotions that have been repressed or ignored: The sacral chakra, as previously revealed, is related to emotions, creativity, and pleasure. As a result, suppressing or ignoring emotions might impede the entire healing process. Allowing yourself to feel and express your emotions healthily is critical, and shadow work can be beneficial.

Lack of Creativity and Expression: Creativity and self-expression are also related to the sacral chakra. This is why you should not ignore or stifle your creative side. Make time for creative pursuits that delight you, whether painting, writing, dancing, or any other self-expression that speaks to your spirit.

Intimate Relationship Imbalance: You already know that the sacral chakra is linked to intimacy and relationships. Relationship imbalances, such as codependency, emotional isolation, or poor boundaries, can all have an impact on sacral chakra healing. Strive for balanced, respectful, and real interactions with others while maintaining clear limits and sustaining good relationships.

Neglecting Sensual Self-Care: Sensuality and self-care also relate to the sacral chakra. Neglecting self-care techniques or failing to prioritize sensual needs might impede healing. Aromatherapy, self-massage, or wearing clothing that makes you feel good.

Change Resistance and Flexibility: The sacral chakra is also associated with flexibility and flow movement. Sacral chakra healing might be hampered by resistance to change, rigidity, or hanging onto obsolete beliefs. So embrace flexibility, be open to new experiences, and allow yourself to change and grow!

The Darkness The Sacral Chakra's Aspects

The Shadow element often shows shame and fears regarding creativity, emotions, sex life, and life's joys in general in the area of the sacral chakra.

The Shadow, for example, frequently manifests itself in the perspective of artistic professions. With the increased availability of chances to pursue and monetize creative interests, some people denigrate these pursuits as mere hobbies and offer bad advice to other creative people who pursue their passions. Why? They usually regret not doing the same! As a result, their resentment transforms into judgment and humiliation, encouraging others to follow traditional career routes and endure unhappiness like themselves.

As a result, many people, particularly men, repress their emotional demands while harshly judging others who express their emotions. These feelings can develop as mental or physical illnesses. In reality, mounting research points to a relationship between emotions and illness, with countless people suffering or even dying as a result of neglected emotional well-being. While society is growing more open to discussing and appreciating healthy and joyful sexual experiences, many people were raised with limited views on sexuality as a result of cultural or religious beliefs. The Shadow manifests as judgment toward others with more emancipated viewpoints in these circumstances.

Individuals who are insecure about their own sexual lives and identities frequently criticize anyone who challenges these narrow ideas.

These are only a few examples of the far-reaching effects of disregarding our Shadows. You must address your concerns if you are ashamed in any of these areas or condemn others for them. Shame interferes with our ability to completely enjoy life and realize our authentic selves, and overcoming it is critical to growing toward self-awareness and having a strong will and self-esteem.

Unblock Your Sacral Chakra with These Healing Resources

Numerous techniques and approaches are available for healing the sacral chakra and treating its basic issues. Once again, the following pages contain a list of many approaches that can help you on your healing journey.

Nature Interaction

Bathing in moonlight and immersing yourself in clear water might help to stimulate and balance the second chakra. Contemplating a natural watercourse, swimming in it, or sipping from a freshwater fountain can cleanse and eliminate emotional barriers, allowing life to flow more freely within your body. Combining moonlit contemplation with touch with water is thought to have profoundly good effects on the soul.

Water and hydration are so crucial for sacral chakra healing that you should also emphasize wet or high-water-content foods like fruits, soups, and smoothies.

Music Therapy

Music: Various genres of music can stimulate the second chakra by instilling enthusiasm and a carefree attitude. Flowing rhythms are especially beneficial in this therapy because they awaken and bring emotions to the surface. Listen to the beautiful melodies of birds, the gentle murmur of flowing water in nature, or the calming sounds of a tiny indoor fountain to soothe and harmonize the sacral chakra.

Vowel: A closed "o" sound activates the root chakra. In the musical scale, this sound resonates in the key of D. The vowel "o" connotes circular movement. When it is closed, approaching the sound of "u" arouses powerful emotions and guides you to a comprehensive experience. In addition, the exclamation!" conveys a great emotion of adoration. Similarly, the sound "o" stimulates our ability to be amazed by the wonders of creation.

Chromotherapy

As mentioned at the start of this chapter, orange is the hue of the sacral chakra and, as such, the one you should use to balance or unblock it. Remember that orange foods can also aid you with this. Apricots, butternut squash, orange cherry tomatoes, papaya, peaches, carrots, cantaloupe, mandarins, mangos, nectarines, oranges, and sweet potatoes are a few examples.

Therapy using Crystals

When attempting to heal the second or sacral chakra, it's best to use crystals that stimulate sexual energy and aid emotional processing. Here are several possibilities:

Carnelian is an orangish or reddish-brown stone that enhances libido, helps with sexual problems, and promotes creativity.

Orange Calcite is a vivid orange mineral that heals negative emotions and strengthens creative abilities.

Orange Moonstone is a luminous crystal that is associated with feminine energy. It can help with emotional healing and hormone balance and improve intuition and creativity.

Sunstone is an orange-colored stone that aids in the healing of negative emotions.

Tiger's Eye: A tiger-striped stone that promotes emotional balance and a calmer mindset while aiding in healing sadness, anxiety, and strong negative emotions.

Aromatherapy

Use essential oils that help balance emotions and stimulate joy, pleasure, creativity, and flexibility to strengthen the sacral chakra. Some good alternatives include Jasmine, clary sage, rose, orange, ylang-ylang, and helichrysum.

Yoga Exercises

The following yoga postures are specifically recommended to aid with sacral chakra healing:

Yoga Tantric: This type of yoga is largely concerned with the second chakra. Tantra celebrates the interaction of feminine and masculine powers, known as Shakti and Shiva, as a constant dance of creation that gives rise to the variegated world we see. Tantra strives to achieve a profound unity with the cosmic manifestation of sexuality by fully embracing life and waking all senses. Tantric yoga seeks to unleash the transformational potential of this divine energy via practices that refine and elevate the sexual experience.

Methods For Chakra Healing And Balancing

You are now aware of the strategies for healing and balancing your chakras. This chapter will go over how to heal and balance individual chakras. If you know that a chakra in your body is not operating properly, you can eliminate the blockage and balance the energy flow.

This chapter will teach you how to use particular techniques to heal the chakras and recommend important lifestyle and behavioral changes. By implementing these modifications, you can expect speedier healing and a better balance in your life and energy. By making these modifications, you might expect faster recovery and a better balance in your life and issues. Controlling your mind and emotions will become easier, and it will be simple to stay stress-free and cheerful.

HEALING OF THE ROOT CHAKRAS

Changes in Lifestyle

Practice Hiking and Earth Sitting

To balance the root chakra, you must build a strong connection with the Earth, as the Earth is the physical element of this chakra. You may feel disoriented when this chakra is blocked or out of balance. Every day, try to be as close to the globe as possible. Earth Sitting is a fantastic method for connecting with the Earth. Hiking expeditions can also help you reconnect with the planet.

Plant a garden

Gardening is another method to connect deeply with the land. Every plant you handle while gardening has roots deep into the Earth. You will have direct contact with the seeds. Gardening also necessitates a large amount of Earth, which aids in the restoration of balance.

Increase your physical activity level.

Excessive and abrupt weight gain is one of the negative consequences of root chakra imbalance. You must incorporate much physical activity into your life to restore equilibrium. It's fine if your job requires a lot of hard labor; otherwise, join a gym. Sweating every day is critical for achieving equilibrium. You're in for a big task if you're trying to rebalance your root chakra while living a sedentary lifestyle.

Try Walking on Grass Without Shoes

Another technique to build a sensory connection with the ground is to walk barefoot in the grass in gardens. It is a calming and soothing workout. This activity also has several other health benefits. It is, nevertheless, ideal for root chakra healing. You'll feel more grounded, sensible, and confident after the walks.

Consume Red Fruits

THIS CHAKRA'S COLOR IS RED. EATING RED FRUITS AND KEEPING RED THINGS AROUND YOU WILL ASSIST YOU IN HEALING THIS CHAKRA FAST.

Yoga postures

Several important yoga asanas can aid in speedier healing and chakra balance. Among them are:

Forward Bend While Standing

Pose from head to toe

Pose with Supported Corpse

Warrior 1 Warrior 2

Pose of a tree

Chair position

Supported Child's stance

Meditation

Meditation is an effective technique for healing and balancing the chakras. While meditating, concentrate on your pelvic region and connect it to your third eye chakra. Consciously expand and contract this region to help stimulate the energy in this chakra.

Crystals

This chakra can be restored using black tourmaline, bloodstone, hematite, obsidian, ruby, garnet, onyx, lodestone, fire agate, red jasper, and smoky quartz.

Aromatherapy Oils

Essential oils that heal the root chakra include myrrh, patchouli, sandalwood, and spikenard.

HEALING OF THE SACRAL CHAKRAS

Changes in Lifestyle

Allow Your Sexual Energy to Flow Properly

This chakra is geared at enjoying the world's bounty. Because the physical position of this chakra is so close to your genitals, the sexual energy in your body can easily become unbalanced. You must properly channel your sexual energy. If your sexual energy is not properly expressed, you may acquire negativity. Your personality may shift, and your social behavior may become confrontational. To keep this chakra in balance, you must have a healthy and vigorous sexual life.

Discover New Things

This chakra enjoys trying new things. However, if the energies in this chakra are out of harmony, you may find it difficult to be interested in anything. The simplest method to reestablish equilibrium is to force oneself to try new things. Experiment with new foods, outfits, and locations. Change and variation will aid in the healing of the chakras.

Experiment with Creative Activities

This chakra has a lot of creative potential. This is the explorers' chakra. It contains a lot of creative energy. It can help boost this chakra's energy centers if you try fresh and novel things.

Participate in Community Service

This chakra enjoys living for itself, yet it can lead to self-serving, unrestrained, and insensitive behavior. It would be beneficial if you participated in community service to maintain your sacral chakra balance.

Take Advantage of Reiki Healing

Reiki treatment is an excellent method for locating and resolving blockages in this chakra. If you've suddenly developed a dislike for things, you should get aid from a Reiki healer right now.

Orange Color

THIS CHAKRA IS ORANGE IN COLOR. THE COLOR IS ONE OF THE MOST VIBRANT AND FLAMBOYANT. IT PROVIDES YOU WITH A UNIQUE FLAVOR AND PERSONALITY. EATING FRUITS AND KEEPING THINGS OF THIS COLOR NEAR YOU CAN HELP RESTORE THE ENERGY BALANCE IF THIS CHAKRA IS OUT OF BALANCE.

Yoga postures

The following are some of the most important yoga asanas for healing chakra imbalance:

Pose of a happy infant

Child's stance

Dog facing downward

Pose with a cow face

Pose with a fixed angle

Pose with an open-angle

Warrior stances

Pose with a four-legged staff

Meditation

When you meditate, you must concentrate on the area right below your navel. Feel for the orange glow there. Instill good thinking and let go of repressed memories and emotions.

Crystals

Orange Some crystals that can assist in healing this chakra are tourmaline, sunstone, carnelian, moonstone, and amber.

Aromatherapy Oils

Patchouli, rosewood, sandalwood, and ylang-ylang are essential oils that help with this chakra imbalance.

Healing of the Solar Plexus Chakra

Changes in Lifestyle

Maintain healthy boundaries.

An imbalance in this chakra may cause you to lose sight of your personal and professional limits. Practicing appropriate boundaries in your personal and professional lives is the best way to balance this chakra. Don't try to take someone else's space. The more you adhere to the boundaries, the easier it will be to live a healthy existence. Your solar plexus chakra will calm down if you reduce your aggressive and invading impulses.

Sungazing

This chakra is powered by the sun and shines brightly within you. If you lack energy in this chakra or find it difficult to focus on your endeavors, try sun gazing early in the morning when the sun is crimson red. It will strengthen your chakra.

Sunbathing

Like sun gazing, sunbathing is excellent for correcting the imbalance in the solar plexus chakra. It will also assist you in resolving a variety of skin concerns.

Physically demanding routine

You must keep this chakra activated by following a physically active regimen. This chakra does not function efficiently in those who lead sedentary lives. This is the chakra of those who labor hard. Try to find a profession that requires a lot of physical labor, or go to the gym or participate in outdoor activities.

Getting out of your comfort zone

This is a chakra that establishes new standards. It motivates you to strive for excellence in all you do. This chakra will become out of balance if you live a life that does not require you to leave your comfort zone and face new difficulties. Take on new tasks to keep this chakra active.

The color yellow

THIS CHAKRA'S COLOR IS YELLOW, SO YELLOW-COLORED FRUITS AND THINGS IN THIS COLOR WILL BE BENEFICIAL FOR RESTORING THE ENERGY BALANCE IN THIS CHAKRA.

Some of the most significant necessary yoga asanas for chakra imbalance treatment are:

Pranayam, or breathing exercises

Bellows respiration

Pose on a boat

Pose in the shape of a half-boat

Salute to the Sun

Cat stance

Cow stance

Meditation

You can repair this chakra by practicing body scan meditation and breathing meditation. These meditation techniques allow you to sense the raw power in your body and gain a deeper grasp on your physicality.

Crystals

Yellow citrine, yellow topaz, yellow tiger's eye, amber, rutilated quartz, and yellow agate can all help balance this chakra's energy.

Aromatherapy Oils

Essential oils for correcting this chakra imbalance include rosewood, lemon, lavender, Roman chamomile, and rosemary.

Changes in Lifestyle for Heart Chakra Healing

Discover new art forms.

The heart chakra is the source of all creation. If this chakra is out of balance, igniting your creative spark is the best approach to restore energy balance. Make an effort to learn some new creative art forms. Listening to music, learning to play an instrument, sketching, painting, singing, dancing, and any other creative manner of expressing your energies can all assist in boosting the energy center in this chakra.

Take good care of yourself.

This chakra may become out of balance if you do not receive adequate attention or care. Because this chakra is vulnerable, emotional stability is crucial. You must indulge in self-care to restore balance. Treat yourself regularly. Allow yourself enough ' me time.' Don't put off your requirements for too long.

Someone you adore

This chakra has a strong need for love. When this chakra is out of harmony, people feel unloved, undesired, and unwanted. Love someone to keep this chakra balanced. It is not necessary to adore a certain person. Put your heart and soul into anything. Love your pets, art forms, hobbies, or the people around you.

Maintain your motivation.

It would be beneficial to keep yourself motivated to maintain this chakra balance. Negativity, despair, and regret are just a few of the emotions that can throw this chakra off balance. Listen to motivating speakers and engage in activities that make you happy. Your cheerful attitude will go a long way toward keeping this chakra balanced.

Perform charitable or social work.

Charity and social service are excellent strategies to keep this chakra orderly. The more you help others, the more open you are to positive energy. In nature, you grow more accepting. This is an excellent approach to keep the heart chakra balanced.

Explore the wilderness.

Spending time in nature is an excellent approach to strengthening your heart chakra. Nature has a powerful healing effect on the heart chakra. It restores the body's good balance. You should take periodic pauses from your routine and reconnect with nature.

Accept newcomers

This chakra is most effective when you are accepting of nature. You should not have preconceived notions about people. Be more welcoming and accepting of others. Accept people as they are, with no qualifications attached. This might assist you in maintaining the chakra's equilibrium.

The color green

THIS CHAKRA IS GREEN IN COLOR. Eating green fruits and vegetables and surrounding yourself with green color will help you heal this chakra faster.

Yoga postures

The following are some of the most important yoga asanas for healing chakra imbalance:

Pose of an eagle

Arm balancing

Pose of a camel

Spinal twist while seated

Meditation

A guided meditation that encourages you to enjoy nature is ideal for rebalancing this chakra. Loving and caring meditation is one of the most effective ways to repair this chakra. When working on this chakra, you must keep your mind filled with sweet emotions. It would be beneficial if you did not generate too many ideas, as this chakra can cause you to envision strange things.

Crystals

Some crystals that can help heal and balance this chakra are rose quartz, jade, green calcite, emerald, green kyanite, and green tourmaline.

Aromatherapy Oils

Essential oils such as ylang-ylang, rose, palmarosa, bergamot, geranium, neroli, lavender, and melissa can help to balance this chakra.

Throat Chakra Healing

Changes in Lifestyle
Don't tell any lies.

This first chakra is responsible for your intellectual and spiritual awakening. It is also a chakra with a lot of strength in the throat. If you lie a lot, your throat chakra will suffer. This chakra does not support deception. You will not only lose the power in your voice, but you may also experience problems with mental clarity. The most important thing you can do to restore energy balance in this chakra is to cease lying in your daily life. Develop the habit of conversing.

The more you talk about topics with people, the more powerful this chakra becomes. Conversations with others assist this chakra in being more expressive. Don't keep your feelings to yourself. Engage in good conversations with intelligent people. As well as the impact of the throat chakra.

Practice the art of public speaking.

The throat chakra excels at public speaking. A person with throat chakra energy will be an excellent orator. However, if your throat chakra is not functioning properly, practicing public speaking will assist you in balancing your throat chakra.

Make an effort to be more expressive.

Begin expressing your emotions. The more you suppress your emotions, the greater the strain on your throat chakra. Stop suppressing your feelings. Speak your heart out, and this will aid in restoring equilibrium in the throat chakra.

Skywatching

Gazing at the blue sky might also help to restore equilibrium to the throat chakra. The light blue sky energizes your throat chakra, allowing you to heal faster.

- The colour blue

BLUE THINGS HELP HEAL THIS CHAKRA, AND YOU CAN EAT BLUE FRUITS AND KEEP BLUE THINGS AROUND YOU FOR FAST CHAKRA HEALING.

Yoga postures

The following are some of the most important yoga asanas for healing chakra imbalance:

Pose on the bridge

Triangle position

Pose of a Camel

Warrior stance

Side angle widened

Pose of the plough

Shoulder support

Meditation Meditation while singing the chakra's seed mantra, 'Ham,' is useful. Even guided meditations with visualizations can assist in curing this chakra imbalance.

The more time you meditate on this chakra, the better the effects. Your first goal should be to make your communication more clear.

Crystals

To address this chakra's imbalances, use lapis lazuli, iolite, turquoise, blue kyanite, aquamarine, celestite, and sodalite.

Aromatherapy Oils

Essential oils to cure this chakra include rosemary, frankincense, lavender, hyssop, and German chamomile.

Chakras and the Vagus Nerve (Chapter 2)

This is my favorite part of science. This is when chakra healing became clear to me.

Which begins with the vagus nerve. When stressed, our sympathetic nervous system activates, and our bodies enter fight or flight mode. This is frequently beneficial since it prepares the body for action. Chronic stress, on the other hand, and an overactive sympathetic nervous system may wreak havoc on our circulatory system, immune system, brain function, and even our digestive system.

After a stressor, the parasympathetic nervous system might take anywhere from 20 minutes to 60 minutes to return the body to its normal rest and digest state. During this time, hormones are still coursing through the body, and the effects of stress are still present.

Beginning at the base of your brain and going via the voice cords before branching out to the organs in your body down to your gut. We'll return to the vagus nerve when we've explored our organs, glands, and nerves!

Chakras and Physical Functions

Even though we will look at physical and emotional symptoms in each chapter, I decided to keep the physiological side of the chakras together with the vagus nerve due to the correlation. The chakras are related to various glands and organs in the body, primarily according to location.

The root chakra represents the reproductive organs (testes or ovaries).
The sacral chakra is associated with the adrenal glands (the immune system and metabolism).

The heart chakra corresponds to the thymus glands (the immune system).
The throat chakra represents the thyroid gland (which governs body temperature and metabolism).

The third eye chakra is the pineal gland (biological systems and sleep).

The pituitary gland (which generates hormones and controls the other glands) is in the crown chakra.

Inhale and stretch your spine, bringing the crown of your head forward and your tailbone back.

Exhale and return your hips to your heels, bringing your brow to the floor.

Extend your arms forward, hands on the floor, or bring your hands back by your sides, palms facing up.

Relax your shoulders and back by allowing your entire body to sink into the pose.

Deeply and smoothly breathe in and out of your body, focusing on the sensation of the breath traveling in and out.

Hold the position for a few breaths or as long as desired.

To exit the pose, walk your hands back towards your knees and gradually rise to a seated position.

Malasana (Garland Pose)

Begin by standing at the front of your mat, feet hip-width apart, arms at your sides.

Keep your feet flat on the floor, and elevate your heels slightly if necessary. For further support, tuck a folded blanket or block under your heels.

Bring your hands together in prayer posture at your heart center, and softly squeeze your knees apart with your elbows.

Maintain a straight spine, an elevated chest, and a forward or slightly upward look.

Deeply and smoothly, breathe in and out, keeping the stance for a few breaths or as long as you like.

Let your hands fall to the floor, straighten your legs, and rise to a standing position to exit the pose.

Warrior II (Virabhadrasana II) is another name for Warrior I.

Begin in Tadasana (Mountain Pose), maintaining your right foot looking ahead and turning your left foot out at a 90-degree angle.

Align your front heel with the arch of your rear foot, and make sure your feet are securely planted.

Maintain your palms facing down.

Exhale and stretch your left leg straight behind you, maintaining your right knee directly over your ankle.

Maintain a forward-facing posture with relaxed hips and shoulders, and look out over your right fingertips.

Hold the position for a few breaths or as long as desired.

Straighten your right leg.

Lift your right foot off the ground and place the sole of your right foot on the inner of your left thigh. Check that your right knee is pointing to the side.

Bring your hands together in prayer posture at your heart center, pressing your right foot against your left thigh.

To help with balance, keep your sight concentrated on a spot before you.

Deeply and smoothly, breathe in and out, keeping the stance for a few breaths or as long as you like.

Release your hands to your sides and slowly lower your right foot to the ground to exit the stance.

Reverse the pattern.

Tadasana (Mountain Pose)

feet hip-width apart, arms at your sides.

Ground through your toes, arches, and heels, distributing your weight evenly over both feet.

Lift your kneecaps and engage your thighs while engaging your leg muscles.

Draw your shoulders down and back, lengthen your spine, and lift your chest.

Relax your arms and let them hang freely at your sides, palms facing forward.

Relax your gaze and concentrate on breathing, taking calm, steady inhales and exhales.

Hold the position for a few breaths or as long as desired.

To exit the pose, gently release any tension and softly lower your arms to your sides.

If yoga isn't your thing, alternative physical exercises can help you balance your root chakra. Walking barefoot in nature (even if it's only your backyard) and gardening can help. Earthing is a method that involves making physical touch with the earth in an attempt to employ the earth's natural electric charges to heal the body.

Chakra Sacral

The sacral chakra, also known as Svadhishana, translates directly to "the place of the self." Notably, this chakra is most concerned with one's human identity and how to deal with it. The most positive element of this chakra is that it gives creative energy to maximize one's enjoyment of life.

This sacral chakra is home to the creative life force or energy source from which one's creative potential is emitted. It carries the energy that will drive you to appreciate life and all the benefits of hard work. Furthermore, this chakra facilitates other enjoyable behaviors, such as sex.

This chakra is orange in color and extends from just below the belly button to the center. A sense of balance in this chakra is accompanied by a desire to enjoy all of life's pleasures without the risk of overindulgence. As a result, life's most delightful events and activities, such as sex, delicious food, and immersing oneself in creative endeavors, will be even more enjoyable and motivating, improving one's sense of wellness and the manifestation of prosperity.

If the sacral chakra is overactive, one may struggle with overeating and addiction. While pleasure is a pleasant emotion, when one begins to appreciate things of life that are damaging to the spirit, their sacral chakra is likely to be out of balance. Obesity, addiction, and extreme restlessness are all indications of a lack of balance.

This chakra's balance can be maintained by channeling energy away from sensations of pleasure and into one's heart. To do so, ask yourself before doing or engaging in any activity in your everyday life, "Is this particular action that I am about to perform or engage in truly healthy for me?" Will it be good for my soul? What are some of the side effects of this action that I will gain?" Taking a step back to evaluate whether your behaviors are healthy and good for your spirit is an excellent way to retrieve energy from this chakra.

When you were inactive, you probably spent an unusual amount of time focusing solely on the most practical areas of your life, such as your hard work and career. A reduced sex life, sadness, and a general lack of creative energy are some of the signs of an underactive sacral chakra. As a result, you should concentrate on energizing this chakra. Furthermore, you can achieve this by simply living your life to the utmost! Make time for your favorite hobbies and interests, and engage in other things uplifting your spirit. Take the time to appreciate the lovely and plentiful treasures that life has to give.

Chapter 7 Crown Chakra - Spiritual Connection & Unity

The Crown Chakra, also known as Sahasrara, is the chakra system's seventh and greatest energy center. The Crown Chakra, located in the crown of the head, represents our connection to the divine, universal awareness, and higher planes of existence. In this chapter, we will investigate the Crown

Chakra's profound qualities, delving into its emotional and energetic elements, finding indicators of imbalance, and learning powerful practices for healing and balancing this transcendent energy center.

A vivid violet or white color represents the Crown Chakra, representing purity, spirituality, and enlightenment. It acts as a portal to our higher selves, divine wisdom, and cosmic consciousness. The Crown Chakra connects us to global energy and reminds us of our oneness with all beings and the larger world.

Exploring the Crown Chakra's Emotional and Energetic Aspects:

The Crown Chakra affects our sense of togetherness, spiritual connection, and transcendence. When the Crown Chakra is balanced, we feel a profound feeling of calm, serenity, and oneness with everything. Meaning in life can all be symptoms of an unbalanced Crown Chakra.

Imbalances and blockages in the Crown Chakra include:

When the Crown Chakra is out of balance or blocked, it can appear in various ways. Emotionally, Crown Chakra imbalances can cause emotions of spiritual emptiness, perplexity, or lack of faith. It can also cause a detachment from one's higher self or a feeling of being stuck in humdrum, materialistic worries. On a physical level, Crown Chakra imbalances might emerge as headaches, migraines, dizziness, or problems with the central nervous system.

Crown Chakra Healing And Balancing Techniques:

Engaging in practices that promote spiritual connection, extend consciousness, and enhance our sense of unity is critical to repairing and balancing the Crown Chakra. Consider the following effective practices:

1. Meditation and Contemplation: Practice Crown Chakra-focused meditation regularly. Close your eyes and concentrate on the top of your head in a calm place. Consider a dazzling violet or white light expanding from

your Crown Chakra, linking you to the divine. Allow your thoughts to dissipate and open yourself to the present moment and the divine presence inside by practicing mindfulness and contemplation.

2. Connection with the Divine: Develop a personal relationship with the divine or a higher power that speaks to you. Prayer, religious rites, or devotional practices could all be used to accomplish this. Make sacred space to connect with the divine presence, inviting guidance, love, and wisdom.

3. Sacred Literature & Spiritual Teachings: Investigate spiritual literature and teachings that inspire and improve your understanding of

universal consciousness and reality. Dive into the wisdom traditions, philosophy, or metaphysical beliefs that speak to you. Consider the significant lessons and incorporate them into your daily life.

4. Nature Immersion: Spend time in nature to strengthen your connection with nature and tap into its inherent wisdom. Take contemplative walks, sit quietly, and reflect on the beauty and connectivity of all life forms. Nature has a way of anchoring us, reminding us of our place in the cosmos, and linking us to universal energy.

5. Energy Healing methods: Look for energy healing methods like Reiki, sound healing, or acupuncture that focus on balancing the Crown Chakra.

6. Gratitude and Surrender: Develop an attitude of gratitude for your benefits and surrender to the divine flow of existence. Recognize that you are a co-creator with the cosmos, and trust that everything happens by a larger design. Giving up control and believing in divine guidance can lead to new levels of spiritual connection and progress.

7. Service and Compassion: Perform acts of service and create compassion for all living things. Recognize the interdependence of all life and look for methods to constructively contribute to the well-being of others. Service and compassion are effective strategies to embrace heavenly attributes and strengthen your spiritual connection.

The Crown Chakra is responsible for transcendent spiritual connection, oneness consciousness, and enlightenment. We may awaken and balance this vast energy center by recognizing its role and significance, investigating its emotional and energetic elements, and engaging in healing activities. This will help us to feel the beauty and connectivity of all life.

Remember that mending and balancing the Crown Chakra is a continual process that necessitates devotion, self-awareness, and dedication to your spiritual progress. Accept the power of divine connection, believe in the wisdom of the cosmos, and let the radiant energy of the Crown Chakra guide you to a life of spiritual harmony, purpose, and profound unity with all that is.

Remember that each energy center is interrelated and influences the others as you continue your journey through the chakras. Working with the Crown Chakra not only strengthens your spiritual connection. Accept the trip, have faith in the process, and respect the tremendous wisdom and transformation that awaits.

Crown Chakra healing and balance meditation:

Find a quiet, comfortable place to sit in a relaxed position. Close your eyes and take a few deep breaths to relax your body and mind.

Bring your attention to the crown of your head, which houses the Crown Chakra. Consider a beautiful violet or white light glowing in this space, expanding and brightening with each breath.

Imagine bringing pure, heavenly energy into your Crown Chakra as you breathe deeply. With each inhalation, feel the violet or white light grow stronger and more intense, sweeping away any obstructions or stagnant energy.

Release any tension or tightness in your head and scalp as you exhale, allowing energy to flow freely and naturally.

Now concentrate on your breathing, inhaling deeply and expelling completely. Visualize the violet or white light of the Crown Chakra extending and surrounding your entire head with each inhalation, igniting and waking your spiritual connection.

Feel a sensation of peace and tranquility arise inside you as the energy of the Crown Chakra intensifies. Recognize that you are allowing access to your best self, divine wisdom, and cosmic consciousness.

Consider a question or intention for which you seek advice or clarification. It could be a spiritual question, a decision, or a deeper knowledge you desire. Keep that objective in mind while you continue your meditation.

Imagine your Crown Chakra expanding with each inhale, allowing you to receive heavenly insights and direction. Visualize the violet or white light becoming more radiant and bright, lighting your entire existence with spiritual wisdom.

Exhale any doubts or resistance that may impede your connection to the divine. Let go of any attachment to the outcome and yield to the higher worlds' knowledge and direction.

Return your attention to your breathing, inhaling deeply and expelling completely. Feel the energy of the Crown Chakra rising stronger with each breath, connecting with the power of spiritual connection and enlightenment.

Take a moment in this level of expanded consciousness to silently confirm good affirmations relating to the Crown Chakra. Repeat affirmations like:

- "I am connected to the divine wisdom and universal consciousness."
- "I surrender to the divine flow of existence and trust in its guidance."
- "I am a channel for divine love, light, and wisdom."
- "I am open to receiving spiritual insights and profound unity with all that is."

anchoring the Crown Chakra's healing and balancing energy.

Continue to breathe deeply and allow the energy of the Crown Chakra to expand and surround you in this state of meditation for as long as it feels comfortable.

When you're ready, take a few final deep breaths and gradually bring your consciousness back to your surroundings. Open your eyes and pause to think about your experience.

Carry the energy and insights from this meditation with you throughout the day, embracing your spiritual connection, trusting in divine guidance, and allowing the radiant energy of the Crown Chakra to guide you to a life of spiritual alignment, purpose, and profound unity with all that is.

Remember that doing this meditation regularly can help heal and balance your Crown Chakra, creating a deeper spiritual connection, expanded consciousness, and enlightenment.

Accept the power of divine wisdom, have faith in the higher realms, and allow the Crown Chakra's bright energy to illuminate your path and awaken your ultimate potential.

What exactly is "Kundalini" all about?

Kundalini is, first and foremost, a sign of the body's dynamic life. This phrase, "little coiled one," is loaded with divine and divine-like energy. The serpent or snake is sleeping there, waiting to awaken and become the divine vehicle in our lives. The snake stirs to life when we awaken, uncoil, and swim peacefully through our bodies. The body's clogs are then dealt with in the same way. Irritations and personality quirks are dissolved. The ability to express one's emotions is improving. We become transcendent in numerous ways as we let the energy of creation flow through us, and life becomes simpler. On the one hand, Kundalini will always be concerned with the possibility of holy energy flowing within the human body, which may be unlocked by discipline and intention.

Second, Kundalini is a way of life that emphasizes your soul's realization of the truth. Meditation, physical activity, yoga, music, art, forgiveness, talks, and big life events can help Kundalini's awakening. It can bring clarity, make you feel less isolated, correctly point you out, and much more when you need it the most. You only need to practice a few self-awareness techniques to realize your full potential. Kundalini's energy will complete the task.

Finally, the Kundalini is an old Indian emblem of spiritual aspiration. They thought Kundalini symbolized untapped human potential. It was about how we can all awaken the source energy—the divinity—within us with the right amount of self-awareness, discipline, concentration, and effort. Whatever its name, Kundalini has always been a way of interacting with a culture's gods, developing latent psychic talents, and learning from the gods' own exemplary lives. Kundalini was a way for ancient people to validate the reality of their gods, but it was also a way for them to understand that actual "gods" did not have to be bound by dogma to be respected and supported. Similarly, modern kundalini enlightenment can show us how to access our divine potential without joining a religious organization. Kundalini's awakening shows our oneness with life, the divine, and the rest of humanity simply by existing.

Finally, Kundalini is all about holistic healing. Kundalini awakening has long been associated with therapeutic endeavors. Ancient Chinese people and medieval and Renaissance alchemists attempted to develop themselves through various techniques, whether or not they named it "kundalini" in their respective cultures. Pharaohs in ancient Egypt would frequently carry their ankhs with them to "heal" their diminished authority. Healing through the center channel of the Kundalini was also a focus of ancient Indian culture. Understanding the body's energy systems enables us to halt maladaptive processes and initiate profound and long-lasting healing, and this lesson appears universal across cultures.

Chakra of the Solar Plexus

Colors that go with it:

Yellow

Related Element:

Fire

Body Parts That Are Related:

Upper abdominal or stomach area

Description

The ego usually manifests itself in your solar plexus chakra. We encounter more social aspects of life as we progress through the body's chakras. This chakra is comparable to the self-esteem-based sacral chakra but focuses on interactions with others. Thus, your solar plexus chakra is linked to your overall acceptance by society or friends rather than your skills assessment. Popularity, social position, and even simply feeling loved by others can all impact your solar plexus chakra's self-esteem.

You may feel lonely, unloved, unattractive, or ineffective. These emotions are directly tied to a broken ego, which feels like it is not performing for others as well as it should. Because the physical stomach is such a delicate organ, there is a lot of potential for physical symptoms in this area, including food allergies and a tendency to vomit frequently. However, if you learn how to correctly balance it, you can confront the world with greater confidence and focus.

Chakra of the Heart

Colors that go with it:

Green

Related Element:

Air

Body Parts That Are Related:

The torso

Description

The purpose of the heart chakra is obvious: love, compassion, and connection with others. The body's center chakra deals with neither personal nor external self-esteem but equally balances the two. This chakra is a conduit between you and others, forming a crucial link between the high and lower chakras. Your heart chakra governs all aspects of your relationships, assisting you in empathizing with others, comprehending their needs, and conveying your wants to them. In other words, it gives equal weight to yourself and others, aiming to foster healthy two-way relationships in your life.

An imbalanced heart chakra can cause various problems in your relationships.

This is frequently manifested as animosity towards others. Negative thoughts about others, such as jealousy and rage, are frequently manifested. You may find yourself lashing out at loved ones or expecting the worst of them even though they have done nothing wrong. Trust difficulties are another common manifestation of an imbalanced heart chakra. You may notice that your attachment style becomes anxious, causing you to struggle to maintain close relationships. An imbalanced heart chakra may cause physical symptoms such as chest pain or heartburn. Eager to offer and receive love, and will feel part of a strong community. This is a great state since it allows you to form deep relationships and feel completely fulfilled.

Relaxation in Steps

When you practice progressive relaxation, you essentially override any tension in your body, forcing it to relax to relieve any worry you are experiencing at the time. You begin by tensing and then releasing tension in various body areas to signal to your brain that you wish to be calm.

When doing this, you should do it in the same order every time, and a good one to follow is to start from the feet up and work your way up to your face, abdomen, and chest. When engaging in this activity, you should ensure you are at ease. Sitting or lying down is acceptable, but try to avoid it when standing if possible because standing requires the active engagement of your leg muscles, and attempting to relax them will only cause you to fall. Make sure you're dressed comfortably, and if feasible, attempt to do so while you're somewhere where you won't be distracted.

Of course, if you're utilizing this as a panic attack rescue method in public or anywhere else distracting, you can do it anywhere; just skip the legs. You should do this practice for 10 minutes daily as a preventative step, but you can do it as needed if you believe it will benefit you.

Your first step should be to take a deep breath. Contract one set of muscles as you go. Perhaps you begin with your feet, contracting them all and holding the tension for ten seconds while inhaling deeply. Exhale after 10 seconds and abruptly release all of the muscle tension there. You will then rest for twenty seconds, breathing deeply and slowly as you relax. After that, proceed to the next muscle group. Remember, you're working your way up from the bottom, so you'll start with your calves. Inhale again while tensing your calf muscles and holding your breath for ten seconds. Exhale quickly and let go of the stress. Repeat this method until you reach the face.

Pay attention to how your muscles transform from tense to relaxed as you do this. Consider it the release of tension and stress from your body. This approach can help you not only get out of a panic attack but it may also help you fall asleep—it is excellent for those who suffer from insomnia.

Obtaining Motivation

People who are constantly stressed, anxious, or depressed frequently exhibit the following symptoms:

- They have trouble concentrating.
- They despise making decisions and are often too tired to do so.
- They are frequently irritable or agitated.
- They lose interest in things that used to fascinate them.

- They are suffering from headaches, muscle discomfort, cramps, and abdominal pains.
- They are depressed and unhappy. They are feeling "empty."
- Nothing seems to make them happy. They are depressed.
- They are tired. They are sluggish, tired, and listless.

When you have some of these symptoms, your typical day will look somewhat like this:

You're exhausted. You don't want to get out of bed, but you know you must. You must go to work because you feel obligated to perform something meaningful.

So you get up. You attempt to get out of bed. Everything appears to be in grayscale. You take it if you can return to bed and forget about everything else. You sleep - or try to sleep. Sometimes, you wake up before sunrise. And you have to start all over again the next day.

How can you force yourself to work out when you can't even get out of bed in the morning? When you are dealing with anxiety and despair, getting up to exercise is the last thing on your mind.

How can you stick to a workout routine? How do you even GET STARTED with exercise?

It IS challenging to find inspiration to work out. But you can do it if you think about it carefully. When you begin exercising and begin to get the benefits, it becomes a little simpler to continue working out.

The following pointers should help you get started with your workout routine:

•Give yourself a lot of leeway.

Don't begin a fitness program under duress. It's doomed to fail.

Take it easy on yourself. That is plenty if you can only accomplish a few minutes of mild stretching. Stretching is sometimes all we need to unwind. I've said it before, but it bears repeating: this is not a switch that can be switched. Developing the mental and emotional endurance necessary to drive yourself to go and develop physical endurance will take time.

- Begin small.

You don't have to join an exercise boot camp or purchase a CrossFit club subscription to reap the benefits of exercise.

Look for modest methods to include any type of exercise in your everyday routine. If you need groceries, walk instead of driving to the store. Take a sandwich for a short lunch and spend the rest of your lunch break walking around the nearby park. This has worked for many folks in my experience. Don't overlook the simple things you do every day. Small actions will lead to large changes in the future. "How do you eat an elephant?" is a proverb I've always liked. "One bite at a time." Keep this in mind as you move towards greater accomplishments.

•Pick something you appreciate or find fascinating.

If you are not interested in yoga, do not enroll in a yoga class, even if all your friends are.

Don't make yourself undertake a fitness program you don't enjoy. You'll probably cease doing it the first chance you have. You are more likely to persist if you enjoy or find exercise intriguing.

There are numerous solutions available to you. You have the option of doing rock climbing, motorcycling, or hiking. Pilates is an option for you. You may try swimming or water aerobics. You can even watch a dancing training video and follow along in time and space.

When you have the opportunity, I recommend picking an outdoor activity. Being outside has a way of improving spirits that you don't get when you're inside. Fresh air, sunshine, and a change of scenery make exercise more enjoyable and contribute to better emotions throughout the day.

•Think about the good feelings you'll have after exercising.

Consider how terrific you'll feel after working out. Feel-good molecules will flood your brain. You'll get an exercise high. You'll be pleased that you overcame your initial lack of motivation. You'll feel like a champion.

Make all these great feelings push you to move with purpose when you don't feel like exercising. When you're depressed, it's not always easy to see those kinds of things. It can appear to be hopeless. It's as if getting up and exercising won't affect the situation, causing you to feel nervous or unhappy. However, try to see the forest for the trees and recognize that what's immediately in front of you may be preventing you from reaching the better state of mind you'll have once you're finished, regardless of the life situations you confront.

•Assign a workout buddy who is familiar with your situation.

A friend who understands your situation will be sympathetic. They will not force you to undertake something you are not prepared for. They are aware of your situation and will not add to your anxiety. They will simply motivate and encourage you to perform your very best.

Join an exercise class and try to make friends with folks who enjoy the same types of exercise if you are receiving treatment in a residential setting. Create a buddy system so you can motivate and support one another.

•Forgive yourself if you fail to reach your objectives.

A workout routine is a procedure. It's a type of self-care. You don't have to be perfect all of the time. Give it your all. Forgive yourself if you cheat on some days. Try again the next day. No one is flawless, and if you are disappointed in yourself for not being perfect, you are comparing yourself to someone who does not exist. Those who accept and learn from failure are the most successful.

•Find the motivation to motivate someone else.

I mentioned before that I prefer to use movies to help push myself when I can't seem to accomplish it on my own. Wanting to be motivated is one of the most powerful things you can do. Most of us don't want to be inspired all the time, which might be our biggest problem. You do not have to desire to exercise, but if you do, you will find a method. It may sound ridiculous, but often, just finding the reason to be motivated is all we need to get started, even if it's just a little. Many of us who suffer from stress, worry, and depression lack the inner strength to simply get up and exercise. That's fine if you only wish you could because it will put you on the right track.

The Throat Chakra Is Known As Vishuddhi.

The fifth chakra is the center of authenticity and expression in the subtle body. This chakra is physically placed in the neck area. The chakra is represented symbolically by sixteen petals, each imprinted with a vowel from the Sanskrit language. This figure is thought to represent the significance of communication in maintaining this chakra's alignment. The space element and the color blue signify this chakra.

If this chakra is balanced, you will have no trouble communicating your wants to others. You will not only be able to communicate with confidence and enthusiasm, but you will also become a better listener. People with balanced throat chakras recognize the spiritual significance of communication in all encounters. As a result, they don't use their words carelessly and pay attention to what people say. We can see their commitment and compassion via their words and the significant silence when they talk.

Living our truth is easier when our throat chakra is aligned. We develop confidence in who we genuinely are and the bravery to conduct our lives according to our authentic selves. Typically, the route to authenticity is fraught with opposition from others, particularly those near us. A balanced throat chakra offers us the confidence to express ourselves effectively and stand firm in adversity. Finally, properly aligned throat chakra makes us grateful for our lives. When we are grateful, our capacity for joy expands.

When the throat chakra is blocked, we may experience issues with our throat, mouth, teeth, gums, and voice. It is also linked to feelings of inadequacy and difficulties with self-expression. People who do not believe in themselves frequently struggle to convey their demands in front of others. In addition, they may follow others without questioning or holding them accountable. Such persons may appear self-conscious. They may have difficulty speaking clearly and honestly and may not be good listeners. People with blocked throat chakras may even lie and gossip while talking with others in extreme circumstances.

A blocked throat chakra, on the other hand, may emerge as overconfidence and violence during interactions. People who speak too much without allowing others to speak or who always want conversations to go their way frequently have throat chakra issues. When our throat chakra is out of harmony, we may find it difficult to count our blessings.

Without thankfulness, we may become overly focused on the difficulties we endure, leaving us sad and resentful. When this chakra is obstructed, we may experience mood disorders such as depression.

Spiritually, the deity closely related to this chakra provides much insight into its abilities. Lord Shiva is regarded as the first yogi in Hindu mythology. He is also known as Neelkanth (the blue-throated one) because his throat glows blue. There are several explanations for this event, but one of the most popular—in terms of spiritual awakening—is the idea that Shiva could achieve a state in which his neck chakra was active. He was able to attract disembodied creatures toward himself through yoga. Consider it the removal of a curtain that separates the material and spiritual realms. An activated throat chakra assists us in connecting with the enigma that surrounds us but that we are ignorant of in our daily lives. This state is also considered one in which we gain mastery of our emotions, allowing us to use them to our advantage rather than making our lives more difficult.

(A 2-second pause)

You will now do an exercise. You must do this practice with complete confidence and composure. Visualize your sacral chakra, also known as the Swadhisthana chakra. The area beneath your navel, known as the genitals, is orange. In your mind's eye, the orange appears like a little dot.

Bring your attention back to your ideas. You will now envision a sexual fantasy consciously and intentionally.

This could be a specific location or situation where you will have sexual imagery. Imagine the dot at your genitals rising in size at the same time. The sexual imagery is strong. You are actively participating in a sexual act. Feel the sensation. Participate in the sexual act.

Do not be scared. Do not be embarrassed. Simply view the sexual picture as if it were a movie. Investigate the visualization. Do not try to impose your opinions on sexual thought. Don't get in the way of the visualization. Allow it to happen. Enjoy the sensation without judgment.

(A 2-minute pause)

Your genital area is becoming increasingly orange. The lovely light has now extended throughout your lower body. Maintain the sensation. If no imagery enters your mind, remain in a condition of nothingness.

(A 10-second pause)

If you can't think of a sexual notion, stay thoughtless. Male and female practitioners will feel different body feelings. Do not react to physical sensations. Allow it to be, and let it go. Suppress no feelings or thoughts.

Simultaneously, suspend all judgments and conclusions. Watch the orange glow fade away in your imagination, getting smaller and smaller, smaller and smaller.

(A 10-second pause)

Remove the sexual illusion with a jerk as the orange glow fades into a dot. Consider another sexual image in your head.

The orange glow is spreading once more. This sexual thinking occurs in a distinct context and location. Use your imagination to fully comprehend this notion. Do not squirm or hold back. Let go. But merely observe the visualization in action.

Examine the visualization objectively. Do not disrupt the flow of your ideas. Three times through, repeat the visualization.

(A 2-minute pause)

You will now investigate the sexual imagery. Do you want to know the answer? How vivid was the imagery?

(A 5-second pause)

Your Swadhisthana chakra is latent and stagnant if your sexual imagery is feeble or you stay thoughtless. Your sexual urge is underutilized.

The Swadhisthana chakra is in overdrive if your sexual imagery is intense and all-consuming.

Both conditions are hazardous to your health. You will have aesthetic, sexual imagery when the Swadhisthana chakra is balanced. Such imagery will not be followed by remorse or a complete lack of pleasure in sex. Overindulgence and underindulgence in sexual impulses are both unpleasant.

(Pause for 2 seconds) You will now feel a different kind of creative sensation. Another way to convey sexual energy is through creativity. Visualize an activity you want to do in your career or personal life as the orange glow expands in your genital area. This concept might be anything, such as a large project you want to start, a painting you've been meaning to finish for a long time, or a poem you've always wanted to write.

Bring the innovative idea to the forefront of your thinking. Watch the notion play out in your mind's eye like a movie. Again, do not pass judgment. Do not disrupt the cognitive process in any way. Allow the notion to bloom alongside the orange brightness.

An orange glow illuminates the thought. Relax and observe the flow of your thoughts. Allow the drama to play out gradually and slowly. The orange glow has spread across your genital region.

Sensuality-Based Healing

Getting Rid of Emotional and Energetic Blockages

Sensuality contains a tremendous amount of healing potential. When embraced with attention and intention, sensual experiences can become powerful instruments for releasing trauma, mending emotional scars, and nurturing our inner selves. This section will look at practices and techniques that use sensuality to facilitate emotional healing and release.

Sensual Healing Techniques

Sensual Experiences for Releasing Trauma and Emotional Wounds

Sensuality has the extraordinary power to fully connect us with our bodies and emotions. We establish safe spaces for trauma and emotional scars to be acknowledged, processed, and released by engaging in sensual healing techniques. Here are some methods that can help with sensual healing:

Reconnecting the Senses:

Take nature walks and practice mindful eating. Allow the sensory experiences to anchor you in the present moment and draw your attention to the sensations that arise.

Breathing exercises and body awareness:

Incorporate breathwork techniques into your sensory encounters to enhance relaxation, presence, and the discharge of buried emotions. Focus on your breath as you engage in sensual activities, allowing it to flow freely and deliberately throughout your body. Pay attention to your sensations and emotions, and utilize your breath to release tension and welcome healing.

Create a secure and supportive environment for self-massage and self-touch, using oils or lotions that feel comforting and soothing. Pay attention to areas of tension or discomfort as you carefully explore your body. Invite the release of imprisoned emotions with gentle touch and caring awareness, and allow yourself to feel a sense of healing and regeneration.

Movement and Dance:

Participate in free-form dancing or movement techniques that allow you to express and release emotions stored in your body. Allow yourself to be guided by the music as you succumb to the natural sensations and movements. Dancing can be a very effective technique to connect with your emotions, move sluggish energy, and feel emotional release.

You create a loving space for emotional scars to be acknowledged, processed, and eventually healed through these sensual healing activities. When you embrace sensuality as a therapeutic tool, you bring a sense of fullness and integration into your being, clearing the path for emotional release and progress.

Erotic Energy as an Emotional Healing Catalyst

Nurturing and Accepting Your Inner Child

We have an inner kid that embodies our innocence, joy, and vulnerability. When handled with love and conscious intention, sensuality has the potential to nourish and heal this inner child, allowing us to reconnect with lost pieces of ourselves and experience tremendous emotional healing. Here's how erotic energy can be used to nurture the inner child:

Gentle Self-Discovery and Exploration:

Explore your body and passions at your speed by engaging in sensuous experiences that promote a sense of safety and trust. Approach these encounters with curiosity, playfulness, and self-compassion, allowing the inner child to express himself genuinely.

Expression of Imagination and Creativity:

Incorporate elements of creativity and imagination to encourage your inner child to participate in sensual experiences. Dressing up, using props, or engaging in role-playing can all help to provide a safe and expressive environment for your inner child to emerge and explore.

Reconnecting with Sensual Pleasure:

As you nourish and welcome your inner child via sensuality, create a container of love, acceptance, and joy. Approach the experience with gentleness and compassion, allowing yourself to fully enjoy the pleasure that sensuality provides. By accepting physical pleasure, you reinforce your inner child's intrinsic worth and deservingness to feel joy, pleasure, and emotional healing.

Emotional Healing and Release:

Be open to the feelings that may occur when you engage in sensuous encounters. Allow yourself to express and release any suppressed feelings that may have built up in your body. Give your inner child loving support, creating a secure emotional healing and growth space.

You create a chance for significant emotional healing and development by nurturing and embracing your inner child through sensuality. Your inner child's innocent and pure nature can lead you on a journey of self-discovery, self-acceptance, and emotional emancipation.

WHAT EXACTLY IS DISEASE? WHAT IS THE SOURCE OF THE DISEASE?

According to scientists, it may take a long time to grasp sickness. However, in spiritual terms, sickness refers to an imbalance of energy in our bodies. So, sickness is another name for energy imbalance.

Illness is either a shortage of energy or an excess within our bodies. Life is a voyage of balance. Our balance suffers when there is a shortage or excess within our bodies. We are tired, unwell, and unbalanced.

Our blood pressure is confirmation of this; if our blood pressure is low, we feel powerless, and if our blood pressure is high, we remain upset. Similarly, if the amount of sugar in the body is too low, there is a problem; if it is too much, there is still a problem known as diabetes.

Linus Pauling of the United States received two Nobel Prizes. He was given the Nobel Peace Prize eight years later for opposing weapons of mass devastation. He states, "You can trace every disease, every weakness, and every element from a mineral deficiency."

Proteins, carbs, lipids, minerals, and vitamins are essential for human health. When there is less or more of any element in them, the entire equilibrium of the body is upset, which is what we call sickness.

Our wishes, you see, are the true reason for these elements being less or more. Sometimes, we refer to it as food addiction. It keeps us balanced when we eat a diet tailored to our needs. However, eating according to our desires invariably results in an imbalance, whether in food or something else.

Extra energy is not stored in our bodies when we eat food based on our needs. Obesity begins to set in when we begin to overeat owing to wants, food addiction, or eating irregularly. This suggests that the body's flaw is not due to excess material entering the body but rather to our desire to eat more, and this desire is not of the body but of the mind.

People frequently put a lot of effort into their bodies to lose weight. Going to the gym, exercising, walking, fasting, and various other options are options. Such strenuous workouts might sometimes reduce obesity, but the mind's desire returns after a few months, and the weight rises again.

But what exactly is mind? What exactly is desired? How do I get them under control? Few individuals are aware of this.

When we consume more than we need to satisfy a mental urge, we unwittingly accumulate additional energy in the body, known as fat or obesity. Then, to reduce obesity, we must all work together.

We begin to devote more time to that difficult task. We become distracted as a result of this imbalance. When we begin to feel inferior, we become powerless. Then, life begins to follow an erratic rhythm. We become victims of various diseases as a result of our irregular lifestyle, including diabetes, thyroid, high blood pressure, back discomfort, acidity, arthritis, cancer, and others. This degrades the atmosphere of the home and has a bad impact on the family.

We have discovered that cravings are the root cause of unhealthy living and an irregular lifestyle. And all cravings originate in the mind rather than the body. As a result, the source of all bodily problems is our mind, which holds these wants.

People frequently say, "I" feel like eating something today. Nobody says that, but my body is craving food today. Because the body is unwilling to consume. When someone says, "Today I don't feel like eating," or "Today I don't feel like working," the mind decides everything, right?

But what exactly is that mind? What is its location? Can we look inside our heads?

No.

We cannot see our minds since they are invisible yet exist within us. Similarly, because the roots of a tree are underground, they cannot be seen.

Our mind is contained within our body, and we cannot "see" it or physically manipulate it. This is why, in some circumstances, after receiving physical treatment or even taking medications, we feel better for a short time but are unable to heal completely.

Medicines may heal the body, but they do not treat the mind. Medicines cannot lessen mental desires or emotions such as hunger, anger, tension, fear, loneliness, and so on.

We can see here that the fundamental cause of all our sicknesses is our mind, which is truly invisible and controlled by desires and feelings.

Chakras and Energy Flow

Chakras are subtle body energy centers that play an important part in the circulation and movement of life force energy, also known as prana or chi. These spinning energy wheels act as portals, allowing energy to enter, circulate, and spread throughout our existence. This chapter will look at the role of chakras in energy flow and how they affect our physical, emotional, and spiritual well-being.

Understanding the Flow of Energy:

The movement of life force energy within and around us is called energy flow. This energy is critical to our overall well-being and vitality. We feel well-being, balance, and harmony when energy flows freely. Blocks or imbalances in the energy flow can cause bodily problems, emotional difficulties, and a sense of separation.

The Chakra System and the Flow of Energy:

The chakra system functions as a complex network of energy channels, allowing energy to move throughout our subtle body. The seven major chakras, aligned along the body's central channel, function as significant energy centers. Each chakra is connected with distinct traits, functions, and elements of our being and influences various bodily, emotional, and spiritual states.

Energy Centers and Energy Channels: The chakras serve as energy centers in the body, receiving, storing, and transferring prana. Nadis are subtle energy pathways that run parallel to the chakras. The three primary nadis—ida, pingala, and sushumna—run through the body's center channel, intersecting at each chakra. The Ida and Pingala represent our dual nature (feminine and masculine, yin and yang), while the Sushumna signifies our spiritual enlightenment and higher consciousness.

Chakras and Energy Vortices: Visualize chakras as spinning vortices of energy that draw in prana and release it into the surrounding areas. The spin direction differs for each chakra, impacting energy flow within the body. The clockwise spin attracts energy, whereas the counterclockwise spin expels energy. The chakras' rotation and equilibrium contribute to the general energy flow throughout the system.

Energy Blockages and Imbalances: When the chakras are blocked or imbalanced, the energy flow is interrupted by spiritual issues. Stress, trauma, negative emotions, energy disturbances, or bad lifestyle choices can all cause blockages. These impediments to the free flow of energy cause stagnation or excess in certain places while depriving others of crucial energy.

Imbalances in the Chakras Have an Impact on Energy Flow:

Chakra imbalances can present differently depending on whether a chakra is hyperactive, underactive, or blocked. An overactive chakra can cause excessive energy flow, leading to hyperactivity, heightened emotions, or a lack of grounding. In contrast, an underactive chakra may have a restricted-energy flow, resulting in exhaustion, low vitality, or emotional numbness. Chakra blockages hinder energy flow, resulting in bodily diseases, emotional troubles, and spiritual detachment.

Chakra Healing and Energy Restore:

Chakra therapy seeks to restore the chakras' balance, harmony, and vitality, allowing for the free passage of energy. Various procedures and practices, such as: can be used to heal and restore energy flow within the chakras.

Meditation: Cleansing, activating, and harmonizing the chakras through chakra meditations, visualizations, or breathwork.

Receiving energy healing treatments like Reiki, acupuncture, or sound therapy to eliminate blockages and restore energetic balance.

Yoga and Movement: Practicing yoga asanas and movements that target certain chakras, releasing stagnant energy and promoting flow.

Affirmations and Mantras: Reprogramming negative thought patterns and aligning the chakras by using positive affirmations and chanting certain mantras.

Crystal and Gemstone Therapy: Using crystals and gemstones' energy capabilities to help chakra healing and balance.

Aromatherapy: Using essential oils that match each chakra to help with healing.

Energetic cleaning clears the energy field and chakras using smudging, aura cleansing, or energy-clearing procedures.

By engaging in these techniques, we may clear blockages, restore balance, and allow energy to flow freely inside the chakras and throughout our entire system. This benefits our bodily health, emotional well-being, and spiritual development.

Chakras play an important role in the movement of energy throughout our subtle body. They function as energy centers, receiving, storing, and distributing prana throughout our bodies. We feel vigor, harmony, and a deep sense of well-being when the chakras are balanced, and energy flows freely. However, chakra blockages or imbalances can interrupt energy flow, resulting in bodily diseases, emotional difficulties, and spiritual separation.

Chakra healing activities are critical for restoring balance, removing obstructions, and encouraging energy flow. We can bring harmony and vigor to our chakras by engaging in meditation, energy healing, yoga, and other treatments. This will enhance our overall health and well-being.

Understanding the significance of chakras in energy flow allows us to take an active role in our energetic health and nurture internal balance and harmony. We can unlock our true potential, experience great personal growth, and connect to the vast and transformational power of the universal life force energy by nurturing our chakras and fostering the free flow of energy.

Yoga Poses For Heart Chakra Balance

The Heart chakra's element is air, which explains its strong link to our breathing and the lightness/heaviness of our chest. This explains the connection between the lungs and grief. The breath is essential in any yoga practice, especially those aimed at the Heart chakra. In Sanskrit, this yoga asana breath is known as prana, which means "life-giving" breath or energy.

The yoga positions listed below are a sequence of heart-openers that will help you activate and tune into your Heart center, connecting you to your inner voice. The Heart chakra is sometimes called the "Seat of the Soul," and "listen to your heart" refers to hearing the voice of your real self - your soul and spirit. Remember, wisdom may be heard and felt deep in our Heart center as much as in the caverns of our minds.

Before your practice:

Begin seated with Anjali Mudra and tap your thumbs on your sternum, as taught in the exercises above. This will assist in activating and stimulating the Heart energy before beginning your practice.

After a few moments of tapping and connecting with your Heart center, be still with your thumbs against your heart and observe your innermost self.

Drop your awareness underneath the bustle of your mind and into the depths of your heart, where you may listen for your inner voice.

To become quiet/willing enough to tune in profoundly with your inner self takes time and practice. Do not be disheartened if you find this difficult initially; this is entirely natural. With consistent practice of stilling the mind and listening in, you will gradually be able to distinguish between your inner voice, mental chatter, and messages from the world around you. The ultimate goal is to see and understand both while acting authentically.

Remember to set your purpose for this Heart-centered activity, perhaps by repeating one of the affirmations/statements from Chapter 5.

Choose the one that speaks to you the most right now. Then, move into the positions listed below. These poses open your chest and heart region, allowing energy to flow through your heart. Many positions below also include backbends, common in heart-centered yoga practices.

SHOULDER OPENER HIGH LUNGE

The primary aspect of this backbend stance is the heart center. In this pose, we point our chest to the sky and direct our breath and energy to our Heart area. This position opens the chest and shoulders, allowing us to eliminate energy blockages and improve our breathing.

High Lunge with Shoulder Opener Technique: Step your right foot into a High Lunge position from Downward Dog. Lean back and raise your arms, interlacing your fingers and clasping your hands together overhead. Lift your chest and open your chest, widening your collarbones and moving your shoulders back and away from your ears. Look up and feel the energy rising in your Heart chakra. Hold the stance for 5-10 deep breaths, inhaling air into your chest and heart and exhaling judgment and hatred. When you're ready, unclasp your hands and return to High Lunge, then Downward-Facing Dog. Rep on the opposite side.

Yoga Poses for Awakening the Body

The following yoga positions are listed in the order in which they should be performed. There are 14 positions, all intended to assist you in awakening your Kundalini and your ten bodies. You must be attentive to your breathing and use each as a meditation stance. You can also use a mantra to help you integrate your mind, body, and soul even more.

Pose Is Simple

Sukhasana, or easy position, is the first pose you'll try. Sit on the ground with your legs crossed and your hands in front of your heart for this pose. The prayer mudra is the position of the hands in front of the heart. Warm your hands by rubbing them together a few times. Then, press your thumbs into your sternum.

Pose of Stretch

Gently lower yourself from an easy pose to your back, with your legs straight below you and your arms straight down by your sides. Bring your heels together and point your toes away from your body when you're ready. Lift your head about 6 inches off the ground and gaze at your toes. If this feels too much or causes discomfort, slide your hands under your lower back and use them to support yourself. While doing so, practice the breath of fire (described below). Hold this position for 1-3 minutes. If you are pregnant, avoid this stance and the breath of fire.

Pranayama is the fire breath. Inhale while pushing your navel away from your spine, then exhale while pulling your navel back toward your spine. This allows you to inhale air into your diaphragm, lungs, and throat before exhaling all of the air from your throat, lungs, and diaphragm.

Tuck your knees to your chest.

After finishing the stretch position on your back, you can go into a knees-to-chest tuck. Simply raise your knees, wrap your hands around them, and draw them gently toward your chest. You can raise your head if you are feeling secure. Between your knees, your nose should be pointed. Use your fire breath to hold this stance for 1-3 minutes. If you are pregnant or have a heavy menstrual cycle, you should substitute extended deep breathing for the breath of fire. Breathe in for six seconds, then out for six seconds. At no point should you hold your breath.

Ego Destroyer

When you finish the knees-to-chest tuck, return to a seated position with your legs crossed. Begin the simple position by returning your hands to the prayer mudra before your chest. Curl your fingers in and thrust your thumb toward the air as if giving someone two thumbs up. Your fingers should only be minimally curled, with your fingertips slightly touching your palms and the majority of your palms exposed. Then, raise your hands above your head and to the sides. This exposes and opens your chest and core. Close your eyes and hold the fire breath for 1-3 minutes before going on to the next stance. Again, if you are pregnant, avoid using the fire breath and instead practice deep breathing.

Keep your toes on the ground.

Uncurl your legs and stretch them out to the sides before you. In front of you, your legs should form a wide "V" shape. Maintain a flexed foot with your toes pushed back toward your body. In this stance, do not stretch further than is comfortable for you. Allow yourself to relax into it and know that as you practice, you will get more flexible, and this pose will become easier. Take a big breath and stretch your arms over your head when ready. Exhale and extend your hands to your feet, gripping your toes and relaxing into the pose. Hold this position for 1-3 minutes.

Take Hold of Your Shins

Return to an easy stance by crossing your legs once more. Each of your shins should be held. Then, inhale and curl your spine forward to expose your back. Exhale by flexing your spine backward as if to expose your chest. Keep it calm and focused if you want a good, relaxed stretch. Perform this stance for 1-3 minutes before proceeding to the rock pose.

Pose on a Rock

Tuck your feet under yourself and sit on your shins with your knees together in front of you to complete the rock pose. You should sit on your heels, your feet relaxed. Allow your hands to softly rest on your thighs before flexing your spine like you did in the last stance. If you are comfortable doing so, close your eyes and slowly roll them toward your third eye. Maintain this stretching stance for 1-3 minutes.

Grasp Shoulder Blades

Maintain the same seated position as in rock pose, with your heels beneath you. Maintain a forward-facing torso and head, looking squarely in front of you. Lift your arms up and gently grip your shoulders with your hands when you're ready. Place your left thumb behind your left shoulder with your fingers resting above your left collarbone. Similarly, place your right thumb behind your right shoulder and your fingers behind your right collarbone. For a few moments, sit in this stretch stance. Then, twist to the left on each inhalation and twist to the right on each exhalation. During this pose, maintain your arms elevated and your biceps parallel to the floor. Perform this for 1-3 minutes.

Stay in this posture, return your torso and head to the center, and stare squarely before you take it a step further. Keep your hands in the same position, extending your elbows to the side. Lift your elbows and trace a line toward the sky with each inhalation. When you exhale, return to your previous position with your biceps parallel to the floor by drawing your elbows down. Perform this stretching stance for 1-3 minutes.

Shoulder Raises

Return to a crossed-leg stance for a few moments. Then, gently place your hands on your knees and relax them completely. Avoid bringing your knees up in this position since these shoulder raises can sometimes result in tight hips that cause your knees to draw up toward the sky. Instead, let them relax on the floor. Inhale and elevate your left shoulder toward the heavens when you're ready. Lower the left shoulder while simultaneously lifting the right shoulder as you exhale. Continue for 1 minute before repeating the procedure. Lift your right shoulder on the inhale and drop it to lift your left shoulder on the exhale as you reverse it. Continue the stretch for 1 minute on this side.

Shoulder Lifts on Both Sides

After you've finished alternating shoulder lifts, you can start lifting both shoulders simultaneously. On the inhale, you should lift them and try to bring them toward each other. Then, drop them and press them apart, allowing them to relax as you exhale. Repeat the double shoulder lift exercise for 1 minute.

Turn your head while you continue to hold the easy position with your legs crossed and your hands lightly resting on your knees. This will stretch out your neck, upper spine, and upper back, providing a lovely, soothing sensation. Turn your head to the left with each inhalation. Turn your head to the right as you exhale. Your head should remain level, and your nose should make a parallel line around your head. After one minute, take a deep breath and reverse it. Turn your head to the right on each inhalation, and on each exhale, pull your nose across the front of you, rotating your head to the left. When you're finished with the reversed breathing portion of the pose, return your head to a resting position in front of you, exhale deeply, and relax your body.

The Frog Pose

This will be one of the more difficult poses in the yoga class. The frog pose demands you to squat and rest your weight on your toes. Your heels should be raised toward the sky, contacting beneath you. Place your fingertips on the ground between your knees, fingers spread wide, and each tip firmly planted into the ground. To achieve a centered stance, evenly distribute your weight between your fingers and toes. Lift your head with your chin pointed upward, allowing you to gaze at the sky. Allow for a comfortable upward concentration rather than lifting your head too high.

Stretch your legs out slightly as you inhale, letting your glutes ascend toward the sky. For this stance, stay on your toes. Return to your original position as you exhale. Hold this rhythm with your breath for approximately 54 repetitions. If this is too difficult, you can always strive for 13 to 26 repetitions. Continue to add to your practice each time until you reach 54 repetitions.

www.ingramcontent.com/pod-product-compliance
Lightning Source LLC
Chambersburg PA
CBHW052136110526
44591CB00012B/1743